A
CAR
COLLECTION
FOR
THE
COMMON
MAN

A Brief History
of the
Towe Ford Museums

The World's Greatest Collection
of Antique Ford Automobiles

by

Brian Lewis and Burl Waits

A/A Publishing, Carmichael, California

A CAR COLLECTION FOR THE COMMON MAN
A Brief History of the Towe Ford Museums

by

Brian Lewis and Burl Waits

Edited by Alonzo E. Meyer

A/A Publishing
Post Office Box 1772
Carmichael, Ca. 95609

Copyright 1987 by Brian Lewis and Burl Waits

Printed in The United States of America

10 9 8 7 6 5 4 3 2 1

Library of Congress Catalog Card Number

87-071328

ISBN 0-940749-03-3 Hardcover

ISBN 0-940749-05-X Softcover

ACKNOWLEDGMENTS

The authors would like to express their appreciation to the following individuals and organizations for their assistance in the preparation of this work:

Edward and Florence Towe

Ernest and Kristy Hartley

Thomas and Andrew Towe

Lewis Rector, Restorer

Dick Ryder, President, CVF

Alonzo E. Meyer, Editor

Judy Johnstone, Transcriptions

The Towe Antique Ford Foundation (TAFF)

The California Vehicle Foundation (CVF)

Membership and Volunteers

All photographs used in this work were provided by the TAFF Library unless otherwise indicated.

Cover Design by Rick A. Spears

TABLE OF CONTENTS

PUBLISHER'S NOTE

For the first time in the thirty-five year history of the Towe Antique Ford Collection, the history of this endeavor has been assembled and put into print. We have used photographs extensively to supplement the text. While there are many professionally produced photographs, in order to ensure a complete coverage we obtained many photographs from the Towe family's home photographic collection. The reader may notice some difference in the quality of the photographs throughout this work.

FOREWORD

Every industry develops its own language, terminology and references that are designed to baffle mere mortals, and protect the industry's sacred ways from casual scrutiny or general understanding. While the language of the Ford Motor Company in the early years was not designed to do this, the average present day observer of antique Ford automobiles is often at a loss when confronted with such period terms. It is here that a little bit of knowledge will go a long way in helping the reader understand the true nature of this collection of vehicles.

COMMON ANTIQUE FORD TERMINOLOGY

An "Antique Automobile" obtains that distinction by virtue of being over thirty years old. The designation antique, does not, however, indicate the vehicle's state of repair or restoration. The Towe Antique Ford Collection consists of mostly restored plus some as-is vehicles.

A "Runabout" refers to a two-passenger vehicle with a fold-down top and side curtains. Ford used this term exclusively to describe this type of vehicle from the Early Alphabet Series 1903 Model A until 1920. The collection has two 1903 Model A Runabouts, one in the Sacramento museum, acquired in 1961, and another in the Deer Lodge museum, acquired in 1980.

In 1921 the term "Roadster" replaced the name "Runabout". A 1921 Model T Roadster is the only 1921 car in the collection. It was acquired in 1963 and is displayed in Sacramento.

A "Couplet" is a two-passenger car with a combination of convertible top and the innovation of glass windows that can be opened and closed. Introduced by Ford in 1915, an example of the 1915 Model T Couplet was acquired in 1963 and is on display in Sacramento.

The designation "Cabriolet" replaced "Couplet" with the appearance of the Model A Fords in 1928. Henry Ford intended that a complete air of newness accompany the Model A's, and most all model and body style designations were changed. The first Ford Cabriolet to appear was the 1931 Model A. An example of this model was added to the collection in 1975 and can be seen in Sacramento.

A "Coupe" refers to a closed car with accommodations for only two passengers. The earliest introduction of this type of vehicle by Ford was the 1922 Model T Coupe. An example of this model was purchased in 1963 and is on display in Sacramento.

A "Touring Car" indicated that a vehicle could seat four passengers, two in front and two in back, and that it had a convertible top and snap-in side curtains as opposed to glass windows. The first Ford Model B Touring Car appeared in 1904. This model was acquired for the collection in 1971 and is in the Sacramento museum.

In 1928 with the introduction of the Model A, "Phaeton" replaced "Touring Car". In 1972 the collection acquired a 1928 AR Phaeton which is displayed in Sacramento.

In 1931 the term "Convertible Sedan" was introduced to describe a four-passenger car with convertible top and roll-up windows. Its only difference from the Phaeton was that it featured roll-up side windows, instead of snap-in side curtains. An example of the 1931 Model A-400 Convertible Sedan was bought in 1969 and is displayed in Sacramento. Another A-400 is on display in Deer Lodge.

"Town Car" described a car that was meant to be chauffeur-driven and had a glass partition between the driver and the passengers. The first Ford Town Car was a 1908 Model T. An example of the 1911 Model was acquired in 1978 and appears in Sacramento. The term Town Car is used incorrectly today to denote a large luxury sedan.

A "Town Sedan" is distinguished from other sedans by its three side windows compared to the regular two. This type of Ford first appeared in 1929 as a Model A Town Sedan. An example, acquired in 1961, can been seen at the Deer Lodge museum.

The term "Fordor" was a term coined by Henry Ford to denote that a vehicle in his product line had "four doors". Its was first used on the 1923 Model T Fordor Sedan. This 1970 purchase is in Sacramento.

Similarly, Ford used the term "Tudor" to indicate two-door models. The designation was first applied to the 1926 Model T Tudor; an example added to the collection in 1978 can be seen in Sacramento.

"Commercial Vehicle" is self explanatory and refers to trucks, pick-ups, and delivery vans. Two of the first commercial vehicles added to Ford's line were the 1913 Model T Depot Hack, one of which was purchased for the collection in 1973 and is on display in Deer Lodge, and the 1913 Model T Express Wagon. An example of the Express Wagon was acquired in 1968 and can be seen in the Sacramento collection.

There are other terms and identifiers used for the classification of Fords, but what has been presented here should be sufficient for the study of the collection and the contents and appendices of this book and of other literature available on the Towe Antique Ford Collection.

Photograph: Introduction.1

Edward Towe's first three Model T Fords that formed the
basis of the Towe Antique Ford Collection. From left to
right: 1911 Model T Touring; 1914 Model T Touring; 1923
Model T Roadster.

INTRODUCTION

The title of this book, "A CAR COLLECTION FOR THE COMMON MAN", characterizes the Towe Antique Ford Collection. The Ford automobile, the common man's car, made its appearance early in the twentieth century. Indeed, Henry Ford motorized the American working man and began a new phase of production that helped catapult America to further industrial greatness.

Automobile collections often consist of the unique, the exotic, those rare items that cause even the wealthy to flinch when they hear the price tag, leaving the rest of us bemused by the fact that anyone would spend such vast amounts of money on old automobiles. This is certainly not the case with most of the vehicles in the Towe Antique Ford Collection. There are some one-of-a-kind or few-of-a-kind gems in this collection of historic American autos, but mostly visitors will discover the types of cars that their grandparents may have purchased for their first car down on the farm or models like those their parents may have driven when they dated -- an uncommon collection of the most common cars.

This collection did not originate because of one wealthy man's dream, the way so many of the world's other great collections have begun; it simply happened over a period of time, and along the way many ordinary people became involved and helped it grow to its current unprecedented standing. Many individuals kindly provided a home for this collection from its inception thirty-five years ago by Edward Towe. When the collection began to outgrow the confines of the Towe family garage, Edward undertook extending the garage and building more out- buildings to ensure the accommodation of his Fords. Many times after Edward negotiated the purchase of a vehicle, he would ask the previous owner to store the vehicle until his next trip to the area as a very practical way of dealing with his storage space problems.

The first auto in the collection was a 1923 Model T Ford Roadster acquired in 1952 and painstakingly restored by Edward Towe and his family. Soon after the purchase Edward began to compete in Model T races with other antique Ford owners. As the races became more competitive, Edward considered his Model T too valuable to risk in competition and sought out another "T" to race that was not as valuable and that could be made lighter to be more competitive. Later this small-town banker picked up Model T parts from his clients' barns and from gullies on their ranges. When several cars were restored, people expressed their interest in seeing them. The showing of the restored Fords as an advertising media for Edward's banks gained momentum and this activity would eventually become more important to Edward than participating in the Model T races.

Edward Towe's banking and other business interests prospered as his collection grew. By the time he was ready to construct a new bank building in Circle, Montana, he had accumulated enough cars, about twenty, to justify the inclusion of a special basement under the bank building to house his collection -- the Fords' first real home. It soon became an attraction for bank customers and special guests who passed through Circle.

When the collection outgrew the bank basement, an opportunity to continue its growth was presented by support from the Montana Historical Society Museum and from the Montana State Legislature which authorized its move to the State Museum in Helena. At Helena, the exhibit proved to be very popular with the public.   Edward Towe's desire that the average American could share his own appreciation and fascination with the collection was being fulfilled.

When the State Historical Society decided to use the museum space for other exhibits, it was the likes of Jim Blodgett of the Powell County Museum and Arts Foundation of Deer Lodge who came boldly onto the scene to keep the collection in Montana and to prevent it from going to Florida. Volunteers went from door to door of local businesses throughout the Deer Lodge community of 4,000 residents to raise the necessary funds and guarantees that would allow the collection to find a new home in freshly-renovated buildings in Deer Lodge. Here the collection was displayed for eight years and continued to grow. When the collection became too large for Deer Lodge, Dick Ryder of The California Vehicle Foundation (CVF), brought to bear his considerable influence, and with the support of a most remarkable group of individuals, two thirds of the collection was relocated to Sacramento, California.

The driving force in this unique story is a man and his family and their associates who have collected and restored in excess of two hundred automobiles during the last three-and-one half decades.   To meet with and get to know the Towe family and those associated with the collection is a comfortable experience. The Towes rarely mention the value of the collection, nor do they subject the listener to egotistical tales about how the collection was assembled. The Towe's humble goal is to expose this educational collection to an ever-growing number of interested people. The museum visitor can see for himself that the Towes have made a significant contribution to the world in preserving for future generations a remarkable assortment of automobiles produced by the Ford Motor Company. Indeed, the Towe Antique Ford Collection is the most complete Ford collection in the world -- every model of Ford produced from 1903 to 1953 is represented in the collection. The basic purpose of the collection is to show the progress of a truly unique automobile company.

In a world that changes as quickly as ours, it is easy to forget that between the time Henry Ford produced the first Model T to the time that Neal Armstrong first stood on the surface of the moon, only sixty years elapsed. Edward Towe took it upon himself to guarantee that future generations would have the opportunity to experience Henry Ford's uniquely American contribution to the development of the mechanical marvels we enjoy today. Edward Towe has provided the American public an opportunity to view the product of Henry Ford's productive genius by the creation of The Towe Antique Ford Collection.

Photograph: 1.1

Edward and Florence Towe in a Model T Racer somewhere in rural Montana.

Chapter 1

THE MAN BEHIND THE FAMILY BEHIND THE COLLECTION

Edward Towe was born on April 20, 1914, the same year that Henry Ford shocked American industry by doubling his production line workers' wages to the then unheard of $5.00 per day and by reducing their hours from ten to eight per day. Edward is a very proud second generation Norwegian who grew up in the small rural community of Paullina, Iowa. His father, who had married late in life, was semi-retired during Edward's teenage years and helped his son start his first business venture, which eventually led to a lifelong relationship with the Model T Ford.

BICYCLES, BARNYARDS, AND BREAKING YARDS

The Towe's lived on the edge of town on two acres of ground which eventually provided "quite a little space," as Edward puts it, for storing old Fords. When he was twelve years old, about the time Henry Ford produced his fifteen millionth Model T, Edward, like other young men at that age, searched for ways to earn money and to achieve his own first level of independence. With the help of his father, Edward created a local bicycle repair business. He soon had a reputation for good workmanship and reliability in the community. He was able to make enough money from the buying, selling, and repairing of bicycles to eventually afford his first car, a Model T Ford. He recalls that he was fourteen at the time. Owning a Model T in those days had been made fairly easy by Henry Ford's constant attention to efficiency and cost savings during production. When the Model T was first introduced in the fall of 1908, it sold for $850. By the time Edward Towe began his bicycle business, a new Model T sold for $265 and a well-used one for considerably less. It was not unusual for older Model T's to be traded for animals, guns, or other items of moderate value.

Edward Towe's experience with Model T's pre-dated his first purchase by some four or more years. His father had owned a number of Model T's and Edward had gotten to know them quite well over the years. Edward began to learn to drive at the age of nine, steering the car while sitting on his father's lap.

Henry Ford's fascination with machines began when he observed a steam tractor while riding with his father in a horse drawn wagon. As a teenager, Edward remembers his fascination with all mechanical devices, but his favorite was the Model T. He recalls that, "I took it apart and put it together many times." After his first car purchase, his mechanical interests and skills transferred from bicycles to Model T's. When he was fifteen years old, he acquired several more Model T Fords -- enough of them so that he could start a small salvage yard. He accumulated and sold parts. He built trailers out of the chassis and power plants out of the engines. These power plants, minor miracles of all-American rural ingenuity, were sold to farmers to operate their grain elevators.

FROM TINKERING TO INTERSTATE TRADING

Edward Towe continued his "business" throughout his teen years. Sixty years later he says, "That great involvement with Fords made me, what you might say, learn to admire the Model T Ford. And as time went along the Model A Ford came out and we played with Model A Fords quite a bit, and then again the early V-8s likewise."

As a young man he attended a four-year college but he did not lose his interest in the Ford automobile. Edward married during his third year of college and clearly recalls that the first thing he did to make money after college was to haul cars or "trail cars" to California to sell. Edward explains, "At that time one could go to Chicago or Detroit and buy a one-year-old Ford. We dealt in Fords all the time, for approximately $400. And you could drive or trail that car to California and sell it for $475, at least $450, $475, maybe with good luck $500, which made a pretty good profit for the 1930's." He would advertise in Los Angeles newspapers; and after he sold the cars he would hitchhike back to Chicago to buy more cars and take them to California again. "I did that even the year before I was married, between my third and fourth year in college during the summertime," he proudly recalls.

Even today there is little that Edward Towe enjoys more than cruising down the highway in his Ranchero with a few old Ford parts in the back and towing a trailer loaded with the remnants of Fords in various states of decay. The search for those ubiquitous Fords has led Edward much further afield than the neighboring towns, counties, and states. He has made two epic journeys to South America -- Uruguay in 1968, and Argentina in 1979. To illustrate just how much Edward Towe loves to drive, his return journey from Uruguay consisted of driving a 1934 Model C Phaeton back to Montana via the Pan-American Highway. The journey from Argentina to Montana, eleven years later, was even more adventurous. Edward and Lewis Rector drove 1933 and 1938 Phaetons over the unbelievably rugged inland route because they had already "done" the

Pan-American route. Edward has also collected cars
from New Zealand and Norway during visits to those
countries.

During and after the depression and throughout the
Second World War Edward pursued a number of
ventures. At one time he obtained a half-interest in a
Ford dealership; he lived in California; he tried to settle
down as a farmer and he worked as a draftsman. It was
during this time that he and his wife began a family.
Edward's quest for a business that would challenge and
consume his energies led him in 1950 into the rural
banking business. Edward became an accomplished
banker and the business eventually gave him the
resources he needed to begin building this phenomenal
car collection.

Photograph: 1.2

Circa 1960: Edward Towe with new acquisition in tow,
1927 Model T Touring purchased in Keokuck, Iowa, and
parts piled high on the roof. The rear curtain tore badly
on the trip home.

Photograph: 1.3

The 1934 Model C Ford Phaeton driven by Edward Towe
from Paysandu, Uruguay, to Circle, Montana, in 1968.

OF BUSINESS AND THINGS

Edward's entrance into the banking profession was influenced by his father's suggestion that if one is considering settlement in one of the small rural towns of Iowa - where his father had spent most of his life - "the three best businesses in town were the bank, the (grain) elevator and the lumber yards." With that in mind Edward investigated many towns in Iowa and a number of neighboring states. The result of his quest was the purchase of a small bank in rural South Dakota which he operated for four years. His previous business dealings obviously helped in his successful purchase of the bank in South Dakota.

It was during his early days of banking in South Dakota that he acquired his first antique vehicle, a 1923 Model T Ford Roadster, purchased in Winterset, Iowa for $75. He purchased the '23 because he wondered whether or not he could still drive a Model T Ford with its unique three-pedal transmission. As his son-in-law, Ernest Hartley, recalls, "Edward said he figured that he had come to a point in his life when he could once again afford the 'luxury' of driving a three-pedal Ford. Of course, for many driving a Model T was no luxury, but it illustrates Edward's feelings about the Model T Fords."

Photograph: 1.4

The Model T Ford's three pedal transmission. 'C' on the left, the clutch that shifts gear from low-high and high-low; 'R' in the middle, for reversing; and 'B' on the right, the brake pedal.

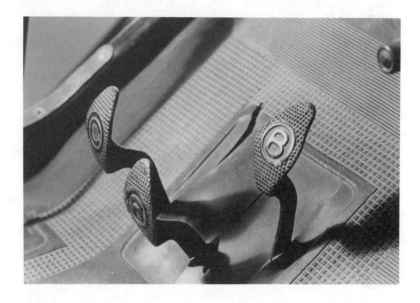

Photographs: 1.5, 1.6

TOP: Edward Towe's first bank in Dupree, South
Dakota.
BOTTOM: The First National Bank of Circle, Montana,
the original building, Edward Towe's second bank, and
the site of Florence Towe's dress shop.

Restoring and subsequently racing the '23 rekindled Edward's memory of his younger days spent working with the Model T's and Model A's.   That particular car, still in the collection, was the seed for this world class assemblage of Ford automobiles. Edward Towe began to collect Fords at the age of forty. This is the same age at which Henry Ford manufactured his first production car, the early alphabet series Model A, in 1903.

THE CHICKEN OR THE EGG?

One can speculate about the genesis of the Towe Antique Ford Collection. The unresolvable question, "Which came first, the chicken or the egg?" applies quite aptly to Edward Towe and his Ford Collection. Did Edward Towe make more and more purchases of vehicles because his business activities could well support this developing collection? Or was his desire to build a significant collection of Fords the impetus he needed to be a successful banker? This is a question that evades an answer, as Edward does not claim any initial great vision or master plan outlining the development of the collection.   It just happened and was a most enjoyable benefit of being in the banking business.

Photograph: 1.7

Circa 1958: A small antique car show in front of Edward Towe's bank in Wibaux, Montana. From left to right: 1909 Sears Autobuggy (owner Paul Renn), 1906 Model N Ford (Towe), 1914 Model T Ford, (Towe) and 1924 Model T Touring (Towe).

THE FAMILY BEHIND THE MAN

Banking and auto collecting are very time-consuming activities, as is the raising of a family -- if they are to be done right. Only a person lucky enough to have a very compatible and understanding spouse in life can manage all three successfully. Edward's wife, Florence, has not only put up with his time-consuming activities, but she has played a very active role in the whole process of seeing this collection grow over the last thirty-five years. During the early years of Edward's car collecting, Florence helped with the restoration process just as did other members of the family. Her special restoration talents are observable in the fine work she did on the upholstery and tops of the early cars. Florence actively researched Ford history to add to the overall knowledge that guided the growing collection. She spent many a day sitting in the front seat of an old Ford dressed in period costume to add atmosphere to a parade or a day of touring. For parades, which were always considered important family events, Florence rifled the trunks and closets of the Towe home to ensure that the entire family was dressed in a reasonably authentic attire. Florence has always accompanied Edward on his trips to buy parts and cars for the collection. Many times Florence's space in the front passenger seat was considerably reduced in order to make room for a few more valuable Model T parts. Florence successfully ventured into the business world on her own when she created and operated a dress shop located in the old Circle Bank building after the new building was completed. Customers would come from as far away as one hundred miles to patronize Florence's shop. She eventually gave up the business so that she could continue to accompany Edward on his many travels. She has always been a significant part of Edward's business activities, holding the position of director or officer in most of their banks; and she plays a very significant role in the Towe Antique Ford Foundation.

Of Edward and Florence's five children, which includes three daughters, Kristin (Kristy), Karen, and Sara, and two sons, Thomas (Tom) and Andrew (Andy), it is Kristy who has taken the most active role in the life of the collection. Kristy recalls that her involvement with the collection was evident even while learning to drive; because the family car always seemed to have a trailer attached, ostensibly because the opportunity might arise at anytime that an old car or auto parts may need to be retrieved and hauled back home. Kristy helped out at the Model T races, and she was also involved in some parades. "Driving in parades, that was a part of life in those days," she recalls. Kristy's involvement has grown even deeper since her husband, Ernest Hartley, took on the role of curator of the collection when it moved to Deer Lodge. Kristy developed and ran the gift shop at the museum and has been a major participant in the daily management of the collection ever since.

Edward's oldest son, Tom, found his life very much intertwined with the collection, by destiny rather than by design. Tom remembers, "My first recollection of antique automobile collections was it was too much work," a sentiment echoed by other Towe children. Tom, like the other children, always helped out with the cars when he was needed. He had to learn to drive these "museums on wheels." He recalls, "I (first) learned a Model T. And so a Model T has almost been second nature to me. I grew up with one. (I) very frequently dated my wife, before we were married, in a Model T." Tom ran as a Congressional candidate in 1976 and used the antique Fords in his campaigning. After his unsuccessful run for Congress -- and again with the help of the antique Fords -- he won election to the Montana State Legislature. Tom is an attorney and was

instrumental in the formation of the family foundation
that is now responsible for the collection.

The Towe's youngest son, Andy, has been involved in a
number of different ways with the collection over the
years. Andy, like the others, recalls his first memories
of the antique Fords in 1955 or 1956. "I remember doing
a lot of scraping and whatnot, sanding and that sort of
thing. Of course I was pretty young then. I didn't really
do that much, but I thought I did." He also helped his
father retrieve cars and parts from all over the county on
week-ends, after the word had finally gotten around that
Edward was interested in any old Fords and parts that
were no longer wanted. Andy is one of the few people
privileged to be a passenger in an auto driven by his
father in a Model T race. He also drove in a Model T
race by himself at the age of sixteen. A printer by trade,
Andy is responsible for the production of much of the
high quality publicity material for the museum. When
Ernest and Kristy Hartley moved to Sacramento in the
fall of 1987 to prepare for the opening of the Sacramento
facility, Andy was preparing to take over the director's
job at Deer Lodge, where one-third of the collection will
continue to be housed.

Photograph: 2.1

Edward Towe at the wheel in one of the many Model T
races he competed in.

Chapter 2

THE RACING FORMULA

The fact that Edward Towe raced Model T's was to provide the background and the motivation that later led to the beginning of a car collection. Among other benefits, it would eventually produce a meeting with a master restorer, Lewis Rector, who shared Edward's passion for the Ford automobile. Racing is a long established tradition that substantially contributes to development and improvement in automobile design and manufacture. Henry Ford was well aware of this in the early days with his "999" and other racing machines that helped establish his reputation as a car builder.

Edward Towe's collecting penchant was motivated by his own focus on racing. The Circle Model T Club was created and supported by Edward and his friends who actively organized, among other things, local county races down the main highways for Model T owners. The nature of the racing that developed was not your leisurely Sunday afternoon cruise on the byways of rural America. It was serious business. As Edward puts it, "We raced for blood, so to speak. We raced to win." Many of the small rural Montana towns' Chambers of Commerce were eager participants in hosting these meets, as the races often became significant local events that helped bolster those towns' identities. The 'daddy' of these smaller races was the White Sulphur Springs race which Edward won on numerous occasions.

In 1961 Edward organized a five hundred and thirty-five mile Model T race across the State of Montana, from west to east, Missoula to Fairview on the North Dakota boarder. The race was advertised in the antique car publications and anyone who cared to participate could bring his Model T and race. It was to be a three-day event. It is difficult to imagine the reasons why a group of Montanans, known as the Circle Model T Club, would take up the sport of amateur auto road racing using vehicles that had been out of production for over thirty years. This was challenging, to say the least, and produced a group of devotees as enthusiastic as any contemporary racing equivalent. The races were a test of speed; and when it came to the annual cross-state race, reliability was a major factor. Obviously nerve and daring, or lack thereof, also played a significant part in determining the winners of these events.

As hopping up engines was against the rules, the stripping of body parts to reduce weight was standard procedure in the Model T races. The drivers were mainly older folk who had had the opportunity to actually own and work on these kinds of vehicles in their younger days. Much of the pioneering spirit of the automotive industry flowed forth in the efforts to improve on these products of Henry Ford's early automotive legacy. Edward's son Andy recalls, that at age sixteen, under the watchful eye and talented hands of master restorer Lewis Rector, he qualified for and won a Model T race, much to the embarrassment of some of the older participants.

Over the following years, the races became more popular and the rules were tightened significantly allowing for fewer modifications. This disappointed Edward and Lewis because they would have less opportunity to tinker around with their beloved Fords while exploring the outer limits of the T's power plant. Edward's collecting activity was well underway by this time, and his focus eventually moved from racing to ensuring a more complete collection. Edward is very proud of the fact that the Montana Cross-State Race Association has continued the tradition every year since its inception, and he continues to participate when time permits.

Photograph: 2.2

Before the start of the first cross Montana race, Missoula to Fairview, 535 miles, in 1961.

Photograph: 2.3

A group portrait prior to race time.

Photographs: 2.4, 2.5, 2.6

Scenes of years gone by.
TOP: A lone Model T Racer disappearing over the horizon.
MIDDLE: Hot competition as two racers reach the top of the upgrade. The trailing car is just waiting to take the leader when they hit the down grade.
BOTTOM: A day of touring for Circle Model T Ford Club owners produces an erie view of highways of the past.

Photographs: 2.7, 2.8

TOP: A break in the race gives time for socializing.
BOTTOM: A win for Edward Towe in the 1967 White
Sulphur, Montana race, in Lewis Rector's 1927 Model T
Roadster.

Photograph: 3.1

Lewis Rector in one of his Model T racers.

Chapter 3

LEWIS RECTOR: ONE PLUS ONE DOES EQUAL THREE!

In serious automobile-collecting circles a talented restorer makes all the difference to the final quality of the vehicles placed on public display. Lewis Rector, indisputably a master of restoration when it comes to the Ford automobile, has spent a considerable portion of his life dedicated to ensuring that the Towe Antique Ford Collection contains the most authentic examples of antique Fords in the world. There is simply no compromise with detail when Lewis Rector is producing a masterpiece for display in the collection. Lewis is like an artist rather than a mechanic. Many of the vehicles he restores literally come into the restoration shop in boxes and buckets, initially discovered and identified by the keen eye and knowledge of Edward Towe.

DEFINITELY NOT A CAKE WALK

Coincidences of life can often be the starting point for wonderful adventures. It is one such coincidence that helped change the entire future of the Towe Antique Ford Collection. In 1961, while Lewis Rector and his wife, Mavel, were out of town on a leisurely trip in their restored Model T, Lewis's son-in-law thought it would be a great prank if he registered his father-in-law for a place in the first cross-state Montana Model T Race then being organized by the Circle Model T Ford Club. Lewis had left the race advertisement laying on the desk in the repair shop in Northern California and had expressed some interest in participating, but had convinced himself that he didn't have the time to enter the race. It was a shock to Lewis when the official entry notification arrived for the race.

Lewis perceived the race as a leisurely three-day tour across Montana with other antique Ford buffs.   He convinced his wife that they should take the time to join the event. It required four days for Lewis and Mavel to drive their 1915 Model T the 900 miles from California to Missoula, Montana. When they arrived at the starting area they were in for quite a surprise.   The scene resembled a 1920's stock car race pit area. There were vehicles without tops, engine covers, and running boards. Others without seats and engine cowlings. Any auto part that could be considered surplus weight was discarded by these would-be grand prix Model T pilots. After they got over the shock of the realization that the term "race" actually did mean "RACE", Lewis and his wife decided that they may as well go along for the ride and at least follow the pack and enjoy the company. On the second day the racing spirit was hard to resist; and with Mavel's encouragement, Lewis ventured to "pour on the juice" for a few hours during the race, much to everyone's surprise and enjoyment. Good judgement and caution finally prevailed. His beloved Model T was being stretched to the limit; and as he didn't want to see it come to an undeserved end, he slowed down and finished the course at a more leisurely non-competitive pace.

The cross-state Model T race was conducted again in 1962. That year Lewis Rector came prepared. He had a different car, one made to really go and keep up with the rest of the Model T racers. At the sprightly age of fifty nine, Lewis had caught the Model T racing bug .

During the social activities that took place before, during, and after the race, Lewis mentioned to Edward Towe that he was dissatisfied and somewhat bored with

his repair and restoration shop in Northern California
and that he was looking for a change. At that time
Edward was farming out most of the restoration work on
his expanding Model T collection. It didn't take long for
Edward to see the possibilities of using Lewis Rector in
his growing organization.

The dictionary defines synergism as the: "Cooperative
action of discrete agencies such that the total effect is
greater than the sum of the two effects taken
independently." There are times in the history of all
organizations and entities that an almost perfect
synergism of personalities and talents emerges to form
one of the great and most productive of relationships. So
it was with Lewis Rector and Edward Towe. The
necessity of having an exceptional restorer to build a car
collection can not be understated. Prior to his meeting
with Lewis, Edward depended heavily on contracting out
restoration work, or applying his and his family's
energies to the tasks at hand. The first car in the
collection is an example of what can be achieved with
family participation.

After this second cross-state race, Lewis returned to
California and was visited soon after by Edward and his
wife Florence. Lewis and Edward sealed a deal on a
handshake. The arrangement was loose enough to offer
options to either party, but contained enough promise
and a level of confidence that each could live with. In
the spring of 1963, Lewis and Mavel sold out and moved
to Montana. Lewis Rector and Edward Towe have been
somewhat of a dynamic duo since that handshake. Each
fully respects the other for his contribution and together
they have spent the last twenty-five years building this
remarkable assembly of Fords. At the time of this
writing two hundred and eleven automobiles are in the
collection-- one hundred and fifty in Sacramento and

sixty-one in Deer Lodge. At the restoration shop in
Helena, where Lewis still works on a daily basis, there
are enough parts to construct numerous other cars in
addition to those already destined for restoration. It is
believed that Lewis Rector holds the distinction of
restoring more antique Fords than any other person
operating a one-man restoration shop.

Edward Towe says, "Lewis has contributed an awful lot
to our collection. He has restored many of the cars. And
he, I believe, looks upon them with the same interest as
I do. He kind of feels like they're a part of his life (the
same way) as I feel like they're a part of mine."

Photograph: 4.1

Master restorer Lewis Rector with the The Early Alphabet Series 1904 Model B Ford. This vehicle is Lewis's finest work, taking seven years and a substantial sum of money to restore. There are only five known examples of this model left today.

Chapter 4

RESTORATION: A FEW PICTURES ARE WORTH A THOUSAND WORDS

The authors felt that the best way to explain the restoration process was to give the reader a brief visual essay of the process as carried out by Lewis Rector and the Towe Antique Ford Foundation.

Photograph: 4.2

Many of the Fords arrive at the restoration shop in
Helena, Montana in very poor condition, literally in
boxes and buckets. Circa 1978.

Photograph: 4.3

Moving large parts around the restoration facility, like vehicle bodies, requires more equipment than a few extra helping hands.

Photograph: 4.4, 4.5

Inside the Helena restoration shop. Vehicle bodies and parts are crammed into the available space and account for many more vehicles that will be restored for the collection.

Photograph: 4.6

"Frame up" restoration is the way it is done, and represents the first stage of restoration. This frame belongs to a 1931 Model A Pick-up.

Photograph: 4.7

Stage two of Towe Museum restoration is bringing the body work back to original condition. Ernest Hartley is shown sand blasting the bed of the 1931 Model A Pick-up.

Photograph: 4.8

The finished product ready for public display. A fully restored and authentic 1931 Model A Pick-up.

Photographs: 4.9, 4.10

TOP: Edward Towe (left) and Lewis Rector in period costume, at the unveiling ceremony in 1986 for the 1904 Model B Ford after seven years of restoration. Lewis's finest and the most extensive restoration job to date. BOTTOM: Side view of the 1904.

Photographs: 4.11, 4.12

TOP: A closer view of the 1904's front end. Every detail of body, engine and accessories is paid close attention during the restoration process. What can't be salvaged is manufactured to original specifications.
BOTTOM: This view of a vehicle, in this case the 1904, leaving the restoration shop means it is not long until the public will have the opportunity to see the result of Lewis's work.

Photograph: 5.1

Henry Ford's personal 1919 Model T Coupe has been on
loan from the Henry Ford Museum and Greenfield
Village, Dearborn, Michigan for a number of years.
Henry Ford described this car as his favorite Model T.

Chapter 5

A POTPOURRI OF FORD HISTORY ILLUSTRATED BY THE TOWE COLLECTION

This chapter is not meant to be an in-depth scholarly coverage of Ford history. The works of David L. Lewis, Lorin Sorensen, Allan Nevins and Frank E. Hill, and Robert Lacey have more than adequately delved into the minute details of Ford's past, and it is not the purpose of this book to duplicate that work. A variety of historical facts and insights from the above mentioned authors and other sources have been extracted and are presented here to enable the reader to understand the significance of Henry Ford's contributions to automobile development. These contributions will be illustrated by references to the Towe collection.

Henry Ford is often wrongly credited with the invention of the automobile. The distinction of inventing, or more correctly the first person to be granted a patent on the automobile, was Carl Benz of Germany in 1886. It was ten years later in 1896 that Henry Ford built his prototype vehicle, the Quadracycle, working on it nights and weekends while employed by the local electric company. Henry Ford's major contribution to the automobile industry was the development and application of state-of-the-art mass production techniques. These labor-saving techniques made it possible for Ford to lower the price of a standard Ford from 1903 to 1924.

These continued reductions in price gave more and more average wage earners access to an economical and reliable automobile.

Henry Ford is recognized as one of America's unique men who helped change the nation's way of life. As early as 1908, the great industrialist Andrew Carnegie directed author-philosopher Napoleon Hill to interview Ford as the first subject in a twenty-year project to discover the seeds of greatness in successful men.

Between 1885 and 1903, there were a number of entrepreneurs who built automobiles. Most of these car builders looked upon the wealthy class as a customer base. Henry Ford considered the wage-earning working man as a potential purchaser of automobiles. This attitude stemmed from Ford's personal feeling that the automobile was a necessary tool rather than a luxury.

PRIOR TO THE MODEL T

Henry Ford built his first automobile in 1896. Shortly thereafter, his reputation as a car builder was considerably enhanced   after he constructed and successfully raced a number of vehicles, a practice that enabled him to attract investors. Ford's first two associations with automobile companies ended because of philosophical differences between his investors and himself.

At the time Henry Ford left the second company, the vehicle he had designed existed only as a set of plans. His ex-partners and investors, which included Henry M. Leland who had been brought on board to consult in preparation for the company's dissolution, put the car designed by Ford into production as a 1903 Cadillac powered by an engine designed by Leland. Ford created a new car company almost immediately, and from the plans he had carried away from his previous venture put an almost identical vehicle into production as the Early Alphabet Series 1903 Model A Ford. The 1903 Cadillac and the 1903 Ford are represented in the Towe collection.

Few cars were produced in the first few years of the Company in comparison to the boom years of the Model T. For instance, only 1708 Model A's were produced in 1903 and 1904. The 1904 Model B was even rarer as there were only a little over four hundred thought to have been manufactured. The mere presence of the Early Alphabet Series 1904 Model B Ford in the collection represents the persistence and force of Edward Towe's negotiating ability. Towe negotiated with a Texas dentist for several years in order to gain possession of this rare vehicle. Lewis Rector then spent several years restoring the car, which had entered the collection in very poor condition. The restoration process involved many trips by Lewis Rector to view some of the other four known 1904 Model B Fords in existence for the purpose of taking pictures and the study of details. After the renovation of many old parts and the creation of some new ones, Lewis finished the restoration of this model in 1986 -- possibly his finest work of restoration. The addition of this vehicle to the collection completed the Early Alphabet Series.

Between 1903 and 1908 the Ford Motor Company produced 38,850 cars. As new ideas were developed, they were incorporated into new models, each designated by a different alphabet letter. A number of these vehicles never made it out of the prototype stage. The Towe collection has representative vehicles of all those models that were actually put into production for the public.

Photograph: 5.2

The 1903 Model A Ford, the first production model in the Early Alphabet Series. The very similar looking 1903 Cadillac is on display at the Sacramento museum also.

Photograph: 5.3, 5.4, 5.5

TOP: 1906 Model N Runabout (a basic car that was popular and financially successful)
MIDDLE: 1906 Model K Touring (a luxury car financial disaster)
BOTTOM: 1907 Model K 6-40 Gentleman's Roadster (another luxury car financial disaster)

THE MODEL T YEARS

By mid 1908, even after financially disasterous experiences with the luxury 1904 Model B and 1906/7 Model K's,   Henry Ford had still not completely convinced his stockholders that the Company had no business being in the luxury car market. Fortunately, under Henry Ford's management the Company was making so much money with the inexpensive vehicles he was building, they had no choice but to go along with him as he pursued his endeavor of building simple, reliable and low cost automobiles. On March 19, 1908, the first circulars describing the Model T were sent to Ford dealers.   Henry Ford and his associates had studied all other cars in production and were able to make several innovations in the Model T. The Company had such credibility by that time that orders began to exceed the production capabilities of the company. By May of 1909 the Company was so swamped with requests for cars that orders had to be declined. Between 1908 and 1927 more than fifteen million Model T's were produced, forty-four of which are on display in the Towe collection.

Prior to 1914, the year that the Ford Motor Company introduced their moving production line, Model T purchasers had a choice of colors. Model T's were now being produced so fast that the paint was unable to dry fast enough. The Company had more orders for this model than it could possibly fill, so rather than slow down the production line, the decision was made to offer the customer "any color he wanted as long as it was 'Japan Black'," the fastest drying color available at the time.   The fact that the Ford was black was not considered a disadvantage by most Ford customers. The Model T was a working machine, semi-reliable, easy to start, and without battery -- all factors that helped it remain popular.

During the Model T era, Ford introduced some revolutionary innovations that were not limited to vehicle design. Among these innovations were the $5.00 eight hour work day, the moving assembly line, and standardized interchangeable parts in the automobile industry. These innovations were developed and incorporated into the production process during the famous Model T years, a period in which the Ford Motor Company made hundreds of millions of dollars for its stockholders.

Photograph: 5.6

1909 Model T Touring, the first full year of Model T production.

Photograph: 5.7

1911 Model T Town Car. While a financial failure for the
company as a luxury car, these vehicles soon became
popular as taxis. This particular car is the only known
example in existence.

Photograph: 5.8

1919 Model T Center Door Sedan, an unusual body style, shows the significant development of the Model T after ten years of production.

Photograph: 5.9

The Flying Quail, the symbol of the Model A Ford.

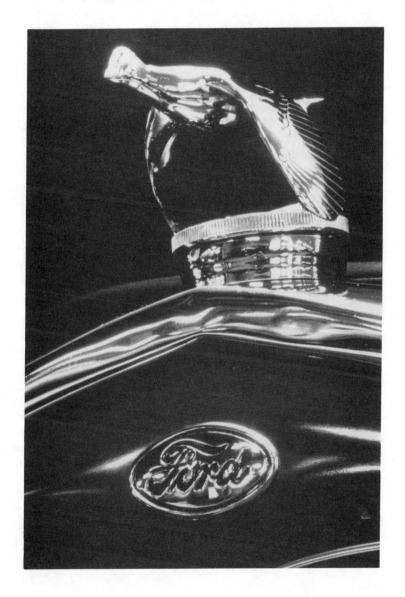

THE MODEL A

In 1926 the Chevrolet Company introduced the Coach Model which featured a closed body and a more powerful engine. These innovations in design by Chevrolet, which improved comfort in its autos considerably, challenged the more primitive austerity of the Fords of the Model T era. The sales records of 1926 and 1927 tell the story of the challenge facing Ford better than mere words. In 1926 Ford sold 1,368,383 Model T's, a drop of 17% over 1925 sales, and Chevrolet sold 588,962 cars which represented a gain of 32% over 1925. When declining sales in 1926 were combined with extreme buyer resistance to the Model T early in 1927, it was evident that the Ford Motor Company was no longer producing a car people wanted. Facing the reality of the market place, Henry Ford went ahead with the development of "The New Ford." As early as 1915 some of Ford's designers had wanted to make gradual changes to the Model T, but Henry blocked any attempts by his staff to supercede the Model T. Ford finally saw no alternative but to replace his beloved Model T.

Henry Ford was a master publicist for his company. He achieved his greatest publicity coup with the introduction of the Model A. The last Model T came off the production line in May 1927. The factory was shut down and many of the workers were laid off. There was a public announcement that a radically new Ford model would be available in six weeks. The public waited and waited as the six weeks passed. The deadline passed, but Ford remained silent. The news writers speculated. The Ford dealers waited, selling used Model T's while waiting for the new model to come off the production line. After a few months, in August 1928, word leaked out that a new model was imminent. Speculative newspaper stories were rampant. Finally press releases and dealer notices began to describe the new 1928 Model

A. The Model A was officially introduced on December 2, 1927 at Madison Square Garden. Orders for the new model flooded company headquarters. The Ford Motor Company was back in business with a new car for the average working man.

Both Henry and Edsel Ford believed that the Model A was designed to be more reliable and out perform the Model T, and they fully expected that its production life would rival the eighteen years of the Model T. Ford failed to see that his own innovations would only satisfy the motoring public for a few years as consumers learned not to be satisfied with anything less than the newest and the best. The forty-three Model A's in the Towe collection, which represent four short years of production, clearly demonstrate that the American motorist wanted more choices of color, body styles, comfort, and other options. All the Model A's in the collection are over fifty-five years old. They can all be started, driven, and move passengers from one place to another with relative speed and reliability. For the visitor to the collection in the over fifty age group just the sight of these cars brings back a rush of nostalgic memories. There is no sound like the purring of a Model A engine. A summer ride with a favorite girl in a rumble seat is an experience that one can never forget.

By 1932 the great depression had played havoc with all segments of American business, and The Ford Motor Company was no exception. From past experience the Company had learned the need to change and to incorporate new developments into new and better models. Once again Henry Ford began to progress through the alphabet designations. Having made a few improvements to the Model A, which included more powerful engines and new body styles, the Company introduced the Model B in 1932. There are several good examples of the four cylinder Model B's in the collection.

Photograph: 5.10, 5.11

TOP: 1929 Model A Phaeton. The long awaited new body
design and refinements of the Model A Fords was widely
accepted by the motoring public.
BOTTOM: 1931 Model A Cabriolet.   The "slant
windshield" of this sporty model established a styling
trend that carried over into the more streamlined Early
V-8 Fords to follow.

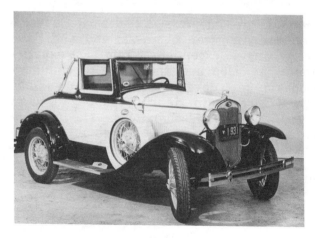

MORE POWER - THE V-8

The Model T engine was a great power unit in its day. The Model A engine was much better, but it still had only four cylinders which placed a limit on the options of weight and comfort. In his desire to greatly increase the power of his cars, Ford came to realize that a major change was needed and insisted on the design of a new engine. Most other manufacturers had produced "straight six" cylinder engines, a design that Ford either didn't like or wanted to outdo. Ford had a vision of a V-8 engine, truly revolutionary for its day and with the potential of delivering much more power than the six cylinder engines of his competitors.

Apart from having a vision, Henry Ford was in a position to insist on bringing his V-8 engine into reality. When Ford presented his idea to his engineering staff, they were shocked and skeptical to the point of insisting that it was impossible to produce a single cast block V-8 engine. Time after time Ford would issue the instructions that he wanted it created only to be met with the same old "its impossible" rejoinder each time the engineers had conferred on the idea. Not to be denied his dream, Ford laid down the challenge that his V-8 be created or he would find an engineering staff that could produce it for him. Several examples of the sixteen body styles produced in 1932 that could come with a V-8 engine are on display in the Towe collection.

Photograph: 5.12

1934 Tudor V-8. By 1935 however, the customer no longer had a choice of engines, the V-8 was standard.

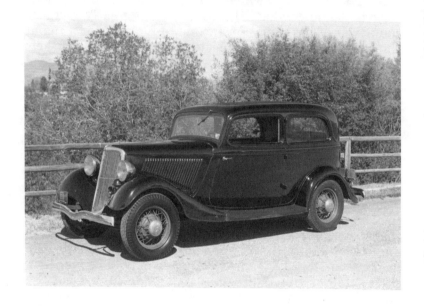

PRE-WORLD WAR II

The V-8 became the basic power unit for all Fords produced from 1933 to the beginning of the United States involvement in the Second World War. This period witnessed a constant development and refinement of body styles and creature comforts in cars that were still targeted to the average wage earner -- a far cry from the basic utility of the Model T. Most of the fifty-eight cars of this era in the collection have been thoroughly restored. A good example of some that are in original unrestored condition are the two V-8's Edward Towe and Lewis Rector drove back from South America.

Auto production was curtailed in February 1942 when the Ford Motor Company tooled up for war production and became a huge producer of bomber aircraft. Though the Company's main concern during World War II was manufacturing military equipment for the United States armed forces, there was ongoing planning for a quick resumption of automobile production once the war was over.

Both Henry and Edsel Ford died during the 1940's: Edsel, May 26, 1943, and Henry, April 7, 1947. Henry Ford II, Edsel's son, was recalled from service in the Navy to assist his then ailing grandfather to run the Ford Motor Company. A power struggle ensued and Henry II won a decisive victory when he took control of the company and returned it to profitability. Henry Ford's autocratic management style almost ruined the company in the mid twenties. He was domineering, and by all accounts many times downright ornery. He consistently refused to let his only son Edsel take over actual control of the company or to allow him to create an effective decision making system that would survive the unavoidable transfer of power when Henry finally stepped aside.

Photograph: 5.13

1940 Deluxe Coupe. A new era of design just prior to the U.S. involvement in World War II.

MERCURY

By 1939 the Ford Motor Company had developed a good line of basic model vehicles for the economy-minded buyer. Ford had also made significant progress in the luxury market with the 1922 purchase of The Lincoln Motor Company. The medium priced car market was wide open. Ford entered this market with the production of the 1939 Mercury. In the first few years of Mercury production, they shared similar body styling to the Fords, but the Mercurys were more powerful and more comfortable. The collection has examples of the 1939 Tudor Mercury and the 1939 Tudor Ford.

POST WORLD WAR II

The forty-six Post World War II models in the collection bring back memories to those people who were involved in the scramble to get new cars after the war. They remember the long waiting lists and the premium prices paid above and below the dealer's selling table.

The Towe collection illustrates the multitude of postwar changes that occurred in Ford automobiles. The balance of the Towe Ford collection contains Thunderbirds (1955), a Skyliner Fairlane Retractable Hardtop (1957), Falcons (1960), Galaxies (1960), Mustangs (1964/5), Mavericks (1970), and Pintos (1971). There are also three 1958 Edsels in the collection.

Photograph: 5.14

1946 Tudor Super Deluxe. Ford quickly began domestic
vehicle production after the war.

THE LINCOLN

During its early years, under the direct pressure of major stockholders and against Henry Ford's own advice, the Ford Motor Company made a number of attempts to produce a luxury car for an upscale customer . Henry Ford was never convinced that the luxury car market was economically viable, and early attempts at addressing this market with the Ford marque proved to be costly economic mistakes. Examples of Ford luxury vehicles include the now rare 1904 Model B and 1906/7 Model K, the 1909-1918 Model T Town Cars, and the 1928-30 Model A Town Cars. While the Model T and Model A Town Cars were luxury car market failures, they were snapped up for use as taxis, a use so outstanding that Ford should have probably concentrated more on the cab building business. As taxis they were literally driven to death. Only twenty-four Model A Town Cars are known to remain today -- making those in the Towe collection quite rare.

The Ford Motor Company overcame the luxury car buyers resistance to the Ford marque when Henry and Edsel orchestrated the take over of the debt-laden Lincoln Car Company in 1922. The original plan was to work closely with the owners of Lincoln, the Leland family, but after the takeover Lincoln was soon under the absolute control of Henry Ford.

All of the Lincolns in the Towe collection are in Deer Lodge, Montana. A notable Lincoln is the forerunner of the modern motorhome, Henry Ford's 1922 Lincoln Camper, on loan from the Henry Ford Museum, Dearborn, Michigan. Imagination can run wild thinking of the trips this vehicle made while host to Henry Ford's guests who included Thomas Edison, Harvey Firestone, and other fathers of modern American industrialization. There are early Lincoln

models including the 1922 Leland Lincoln Sedan, 1923
Sedan, 1925 Doctor's Coupe, and the remarkable 1926
Dual Cowl Phaeton.   There are also Lincoln Zephyrs,
which are powered by the first V-12 engine used by Ford.

Shortly before the Second World War, plans for the
Lincoln Continental were developed and this model was
first produced in 1941. Examples of the 1946 and 1947
Lincoln Continentals are in the collection along with at
least fifteen other Lincolns.   These luxurious designs
were in direct response to the need to compete directly
with Cadillac, Chrysler, Oldsmobile, and Packard.

Photograph: 5.15, 5.16

TOP: (Left) 1926 Lincoln Dual Cowl Phaeton, produced four years after Ford took over the company. (Right) 1931 Model A Deluxe Phaeton, Ford's top-of-the-line at the time.
BOTTOM: 1936 Lincoln Zephyr shows the radical body style changes in Lincolns in just ten years.

AN OVERVIEW OF THE COLLECTION

The oldest cars in the Towe collection are the 1903's - two Fords and one Cadillac, all of which were taken from the same basic plans mentioned earlier. The newest car in the collection is a 1978 Thunderbird. Representing the seventy-five years in between are two hundred and eight historically significant examples of Ford's automotive accomplishments.

These Fords exemplify the eras they represent. The Early Alphabet Series show motor cars that were developed by a stubborn middle aged man with a dream. The Model T represents a bridge between the horse and buggy days and modern automotive transport. The fifteen million model T's produced and sold attest the acceptance of this simple, functional automobile by the American public. The Model A's and B's represent the ability of a giant corporation to accommodate change when the customer's transportation demands became more sophisticated. The Early V-8's are evidence of further adaptability, and the changes initiated by the A's and B's formed the basis of survival for the company through the fifties. The V-8's were also a clear indication that the public demanded vehicles capable of reliable long-distance transportation over an expanding and sophisticated national highway system. Post World War II Fords are generally not considered antiques even though they fall into the over-thirty-years-old category. There are enough cars in the collection to clearly represent most achievements of the Ford Motor Company through 1978.

In the next ten years it is reasonable to expect that several million people will have the opportunity to view the Towe Antique Ford Collection at its new location in Sacramento, California and its continuing home in Deer Lodge, Montana. Each visitor will come away from the collection with a keen sense of American automotive history, especially as it relates to Henry Ford and The Ford Motor Company.

Edward Towe, his hardworking family, and master restorer Lewis Rector, can be justifiably proud of their contribution to the preservation of American automotive history .

Photograph: 5.17

1958 Edsel. First year model of its short and unsuccessful three year life.

Photograph: 6.1

The new bank building in Circle, Montana, the first real
home of the antique Fords. (See the museum in the
basement?)

Chapter 6

THE GENESIS OF A COLLECTION

The Towe Antique Ford Collection has grown to over two hundred and ten cars in thirty-five years, an average acquisition rate of about one car every other month; and there is no sign that this growth will abate. As an aid in gauging the growth of the collection one can look at each stage or home of the collection. These milestones are convenient indicators of the growth.

CIRCLE, MONTANA

In 1954, Edward Towe received an offer that he could not refuse and sold his small South Dakota bank. He subsequently purchased another small bank in Circle, Montana. The second year that he was in Montana he bought another Model T Ford. Then another. Racing was the early impetus for collecting these cars. The 1923 was restored and other "show" cars accumulated; the beginnings of a collection of Fords was imminent.

As the collection grew, storage became a significant problem as the collection threatened to overflow the Towe's own accommodations. Edward's proclivity for growth was not limited to the Ford collection. His banking acumen developed; and as other small rural banks became available, he expanded his business activities and began "collecting" banks. These other banks gave him the opportunity to display his cars to the public. A Towe Antique Ford with the local small town bank's name on the side was an entry in many a small-town parade in rural Montana during the 1950's and 1960's.

Edward Towe received much pleasure from watching the delight of others as they surveyed his historic vehicles. He loved the work of collecting and restoring these cars and he seemed to obtain a vicarious satisfaction as he realized that others also enjoyed viewing the autos. When Edward decided in 1960 to build a new bank building in Circle he realized that this structure might also provide a place to display his auto collection. When plans were being developed for the new bank offices, Edward made certain that there was enough room in the basement to house the antique Fords. This basement became the first real home of the Towe Antique Ford Collection. An elevator had to be installed so the cars could be lowered into the basement. The elevator was constructed from an old garage hoist. Many of the vehicles barely fit into the lift for the slow descent to the basement of the bank. There were two stairways going down to the basement that allowed Edward to take people in and out and show them the cars. Seeing the old cars in the basement of the Circle bank was something people enjoyed for many years. Approximately twenty-eight cars could be displayed in the show room and it was soon filled. Again the barns and garages of the Towe's Circle home began to fill with more acquisitions after the bank basement had reached its limit.

HELENA, MONTANA

In 1965 Edward and the family were faced with the challenge of finding a new and larger display area for the Fords. The bank basement in Circle was filled and the collection was growing at a steady pace. It was inevitable that sooner or later this growing collection should be made more available to the public. "At this time," Edward explains, "the State of Montana approached us and wondered if we might like to bring our Ford collection, which was becoming noted around the country, to Helena, Montana, the state capitol, and put them in the state museum." While somewhat flattered that the state would make such an approach, Edward and the family set about seriously considering the pros and cons of such a move to the other side of the state. One immediate problem facing such a move was that the state museum didn't have enough space to accommodate the twenty-eight cars that were on display in the bank basement, let alone the dozen or so that had already accumulated in the shop.

In a bold effort to overcome the space problem, the curator of the state museum took Edward and his wife to the state legislature. They proposed that the Towe's would make their Ford collection available to the state for display if the legislature would appropriate enough money to build an additional room onto the state museum building to house the cars. This plan was proposed by the museum staff, not the Towe's; and there is some feeling in retrospect that the collection was used by the museum administration to influence the legislature to finance a museum addition which it would not otherwise have done.

The idea of building an annex to the museum to house the Towe Ford collection, according to Edward, "went over tremendously well. There was only one dissenter in both state houses, one Senator, to the appropriation of $500,000 to build this addition to the state museum; and it was quite an elaborate addition." Before the addition was completed, the museum administration decided that it was too nice a space to devote to auto display. So without consulting the Towe's, the museum authorities decided to put a partition down the middle of the new annex and reserve half of it for paintings by Charles M. Russell and half of it for the car collection -- a disappointment to the family, to say the least. Fortunately, the overwhelming consideration that the cars would be seen by more people still remained so important to the Towe's that the move to the state museum was still undertaken with the extremely valuable volunteer assistance of the Montana Pioneer and Classic Auto Club.

It would require several years for the annex to be completed, so arrangements were made to move the collection temporarily into a separate building that was specially renovated to accommodate the collection. The structure, located on Helena Avenue near the railroad depot, several blocks from the capitol, opened with thirty-five cars. "It was really an exciting day in Helena, Montana, with that unveiling," remembers Ernest Hartley, Curator of the Towe Antique Ford Collection of Sacramento.

The museum annex completed, a grand opening was held in August 1967. The divided annex could display only thirty-two of the Towe's Ford collection which had by then increased to almost sixty. These Towe Fords were shown in the annex for ten years, when in 1977 the museum directors decided that the cars had been on display long enough; they wanted the space for new exhibits.

Photograph: 6.2, 6.3

TOP: Edward Towe outside the Helena Ave., Helena,
Montana temporary facility before the annex to the State
Historical Society Museum was completed.
BOTTOM: Inside the Helena Ave. facility.

Photograph: 6.4

The Fords as displayed and viewed from raised
walkways inside the permanent State Historical Society
Annex in Helena, Montana.

DEER LODGE, MONTANA

The old adage that when a window is closed a door is opened somewhere else seems always to apply to the collection. The Montana State Museum administration's decision of 1967 to no longer display the Fords placed the Towe's once again in the position of having to find a new home for the collection. By this time a complete restoration facility had been established for Lewis Rector in Helena. Edward's quest for new acquisitions and Lewis's love of Ford cars and authentic restoration guaranteed that the collection would not only keep growing, but the quality would improve as they began to fill the gaps with the rare models to complete the collection. Edward recalls, "We started looking in California. We started looking in Florida. We almost bought a going, operating museum in Florida, south of Disney World about thirty or so miles. As a matter of fact we were within $10,000 of buying it. And then during that negotiation, a delegation from Deer Lodge came to see me about bringing the cars over to Deer Lodge to put them in the old Montana Territorial Prison which was being vacated."

Ernest Hartley relates:
"This delegation (of Deer Lodgians) was headed up by Jim Blodgett from Deer Lodge, who was both the deputy warden of Montana State Prison and the President of the Powell County Museum and Arts Foundation. Jim Blodgett was a native son of Deer Lodge who had worked in the prison since he was a teenager and was very interested in history. The Powell County Museum and Arts Foundation was in the process of making arrangements to take over the old Montana State Prison (to make a museum out of it) as soon as the state vacated it in favor of a new prison being built west of town. They were acquiring seven acres of land and a wonderful old historical structure. But they

also were getting as a part of that acquisition a number of prison warehouse buildings which were reasonably good buildings but for which they had no real purpose. And when Jim Blodgett saw in the paper here was this wonderful car collection, which even at that time was considered the world's most complete collection of antique Ford cars, (he) called Mr. Towe to see if he would be interested in exhibiting his cars in the old Montana prison. As a result of that phone call, negotiations commenced and an arrangement was made whereby the Powell County Museum and Arts Foundation would provide a home and do all the work of renovating a museum (to provide) a suitable place to exhibit the cars. Then the arrangements were made for that move to Deer Lodge, which was only fifty five miles from Helena versus twenty five hundred miles to Central Florida."

The relocation to Deer Lodge was considered a major move forward, as the prison facility would provide a home with ample space to grow without the added expense of having to purchase or build an entire museum. The Powell County Museum agreed to run the prison facility and to provide a lease payment to Edward Towe for the presence of the cars. The Towe family was relieved of the responsibilities of running the museum in the initial phase; and more importantly, the cars were to be on public display. A ten year agreement was signed with Deer Lodge in 1977.

Photograph: 6.5

The 1903 Model A on the road from Helena, Montana to rural Deer Lodge, Montana, aptly indicated by the cowboy, when the collection was relocated in 1977.

Photograph: 6.6, 6.7

TOP: One of the many stops at Mc Donald Pass on the Continental Divide, by the dozens of convoys that moved the collection, before the descent into Deer Lodge.
BOTTOM: The final exit at the end of the fifty-five mile journey from Helena to Deer Lodge, Montana.

Photograph: 6.8

Edward Towe and local Deer Lodge officials at the
opening ceremonies on June 28, 1978. From left to right:
Edward Towe, Lewis Rector, Jim Blodgett, and the late
Mayor John Wilson.

Photograph: 7.1 (All photographs in Chapter Seven are courtesy of Thom Brommerich)

Antique Fords, piled high on auto transporters, provided a unique sight to onlookers as they traverse the final interchange before arriving at the Sacramento facility.

Chapter 7

THE MOVE TO SACRAMENTO

This big event is best described in an eye witness account by free-lance auto writer Margie Weybright's article in the October/November 1986 issue of the California Vehicle Foundation Magazine. The article reads:

> Saturday, September 27, 1986 is a day that will long be remembered in automotive and Sacramento history, and in the hearts and minds of all those people lucky enough to be part of it.
>
> The day dawned bright, clear and sunny - in Sacramento. Donner summit on Highway 80 was an entirely different story. Snow storm. Blizzard conditions. Road closures. Chain requirements. And thirteen open Hadley Auto Transport car carriers, with 89 Towe Fords on them waiting in Sparks, Nevada.
>
> God had been with them and their valiant drivers over the hundreds of miles and often adverse driving conditions on the trek from Deer Lodge, Montana to Sparks. In fact, the lead carrier of the convoy made it to Sparks only eight minutes past the original estimated time of arrival. And the three individually driven Fords (1933 and 1935 Phaetons and a 1936 Roadster) were only ten minutes behind the last of the transporters.
>
> An anxiously awaited phone call from Sparks reached the CVF Towe Ford Museum shortly after 8:00am. The decision had been made. They'd go for it! Dozens of local car club enthusiasts joined the procession at Sierra College Boulevard, Rocklin, to make the final leg of the trip into Sacramento.

An estimated 1,000 people stood in the parking lot and street in front of the museum waiting, looking hoping - straining to be the first one to spot the 1933 Ford that was the lead car in this huge parade of automotive history. A ll of a sudden, at about 12:30pm, it was there! Up on the freeway, to the east of Front St., came an old blue Ford. Behind it, two more Fords, then a huge open car carrier, loaded with bright, shiny, vintage Fords! Behind that, another, and another, and another. Shouts, cheers, and applause, and squeals of joy were almost deafening. People jumped up and down. friends and strangers alike shook hands, hugged, kissed and danced in the street. Someone shouted "Look over there!" and pointed to the southwest. As the convoy crossed the river, one could see them again - the little old Fords followed by those big, beautiful and, oh so welcome car carriers loaded with their precious cargo!   To stand there in front of the museum and see, as far as the eye could see in both directions, all those cars; the feel the excitement and energy and joy of the crowd, to be part of this wonderful event, was a thrill really beyond compare - beyond words.

It was so moving--looking around, one could see very few dry eyes. (In fact, it is very difficult to remain   dry-eyed   as   I   write   this--just remembering.) The last of the Hadley carriers wasn't quite out of sight on the freeway when the little blue Ford came chugging down Front Street. Talk about cheers! As it rounded the corner into the parking lot in front of the crowd, a World War I cannon fired a welcoming volley. Slowly, Front Street filled with the thirteen car carriers with a total of eighty-eight Fords (+ one Chevrolet) spanning the years from 1912 to 1970. As each carrier pulled in, the shouts and applause got louder and more intense. The drivers waived and grinned. They knew that they too were part of history. They could feel the love and thanks and knew that the cheers were for them as well as for the Fords and Mr. Hadley's generous donation (equal to $100,000.)

The carriers were finally in the lot and the unloading process began. With the care of a mother for her first-born, the Hadley drivers eased each car off its ramps. Volunteers pushed, steered, and positioned the Fords to be pushed, again, up the ramp into the museum. (I was fortunate enough to be a passenger in a 1931 Model A Cabriolet on one such trip!) Lucky volunteers actually got to get in the cars and guide them to their spots inside the building. As each car entered the museum, it was introduced by year and model.

By about 4:30pm, the last car was safely inside its new home. The band was gone, the clowns had departed, the raffle prizes had been collected and the soft drink and souvenir sellers were packing up. The press and local dignitaries, along with the film makers and photographers were gone. The hardworking drivers finally got to sit down and have a late lunch. Several dozen very tied and proud volunteers stood around congratulating themselves and each other (deservedly so!) on a job well done...reluctant to leave.

The day was over. But it wasn't really over. That day, September 27, 1986, will live on and on in Sacramento history; in automotive history; and most especially, in the hearts and memory of all of us who were there and witness to the changing of "The Fords are Coming" to "The Fords are HERE!!!"

The Towe Antique Ford Collection seems to have a destiny all of its own. Whenever there was a need to expand its housing, doors opened and an opportunity for expansion presented itself. From the humble beginnings of being parked in front of rural banks and being shown in small-town parades, to its first real home in a specially built bank basement, across the state to the Montana State Museum, then fifty miles south west to an old territorial prison at Deer Lodge, two-thirds of the collection has finally come to Sacramento, California. Along the way the collection has become more complete, and an ever growing number of people are able to see this unique collection of American history. The collection itself has now developed its own momentum and will continue to pursue and complete its destiny of being the most complete visual display of the history of one automobile company -- a company built by one strong man, Henry Ford.

The California Vehicle Foundation (CVF) was conceived out of a desire to display automobiles to the public in some organized and significant manner. As one speculates about the strong forces that have influenced this collection and shaped its nature and its future, the partnership with the CVF was the next logical step in the collection's future. The CVF was uniquely designed and positioned to work with the Towe family to show the collection in a major metropolitan area.

The two founders of the California Vehicle Foundation, Dick Ryder, who owns a number of antique Pierce Arrow cars, and Burl Waits, an implementation activist, shared a dream that someday they would be involved in a public automobile display in Sacramento. This dream formed the basis for the incorporation of the CVF in 1982. The founders and other dedicated Sacramento area car enthusiasts spent four years laying the groundwork for a museum. The arrangement with the Towe Antique Ford Foundation has enabled them to accomplish their goal ahead of schedule.

On May 1, 1987, the two founders, along with four hundred other highly-energized Northern Californians, including old car enthusiasts, politicians, CVF members, and volunteers and representatives from the business community, found themselves in the middle of a party to celebrate the opening of the Sacramento Towe Ford Museum. This was almost five years to the day from the time the two founders began discussing their visions of a major Sacramento automobile collection.

The CVF was also designed to actively encourage the involvement of the layman in the car collecting world - a grass-roots organization in the truest sense. It was this grass-roots structure that enabled the fast and positive response when the Towe Antique Ford Collection was offered to the people of Sacramento and of Northern California. Hundreds, if not thousands, of interested and active Northern Californians joined together in supporting this organization. It is an interesting parallel that in the early days of the Model T Ford, the Ford Motor Company actively encouraged the formation of car clubs. These clubs helped the average car owner to better know his vehicle in the good company of other owners who shared an interest in the Model T. The CVF membership draws much strength from local car club members who continue this automotive tradition.

Many thousands of "people" hours were donated by CVF volunteers during the year of extensive planning and preparation preceding the opening of the Sacramento facility. It is of interest to note that as the collection has moved to different locations, the numbers of people involved has steadily grown. The Towe family presence is now felt in Sacramento, as they share the treasures of their collection with the public in this new West Coast location.

Photograph: 7.2, 7.3

TOP: A Hadley Auto Transport truck pulls into the Sacramento facility.
BOTTOM: Four transports lined up awaiting unloading.

Chapter 8

THE FUTURE OF THE COLLECTION

It is a certainty that as long as Edward Towe is able, he will accumulate more Fords for the collection. As much of his past collecting coincided with the banking business, we probably should expect a few more Fords to be added in the near future, as Edward is back in the banking business once again. He recently had to take back a bank that he sold some years ago. The energy level of this seventy-three year old man would put most younger men to shame.

Like Henry Ford, Edward Towe has a deep sense of history, as shown by his intense efforts in tracing his Norwegian heritage and also by his clear foresight in the planning that will protect this unique automobile collection. The devastation that struck the famous Harrah's collection on the death of Bill Harrah -- the breakup and disposal of a large number of vehicles -- can never happen to the Towe collection. In 1977 the Towe family assured the permanence of the collection by transferring title to the cars to The Towe Antique Ford Foundation, a non-profit, tax-exempt corporation. This public-spirited concept will assure that the collection can continue to grow and be more accessible to the public.

The assurance of the future of this collection goes even further if one looks at the lives of some Towe family members. Kristy Hartley, Edward's middle daughter, actively adopted an interest in the collection while it was growing. Her husband, Ernest Hartley, developed a connection with the collection that profoundly changed his career direction. Ernest was introduced to the collection during summer breaks from college and spent some time assisting Lewis Rector in the restoration shop. A string of events changed his occupation from teaching to Director of the Deer Lodge Museum. He was so successful during the eight years in Deer Lodge, that Edward recommended that he be put in charge of the Sacramento facility. Under the tutelage of Edward Towe and Lewis Rector, Ernest has acquired a vast knowledge of Henry Ford's accomplishments and a full understanding of the intricacies of authentic antique vehicle restoration. This combined wealth of information that he successfully utilized in the Deer Lodge facility is now being incorporated into the training of the docents for the Sacramento facility. So for the first time in California, the complete history of the collection, along with Henry Ford's legacy to the industrialized world, will be entrusted to a larger group of active individuals who have taken it upon themselves to preserve and protect this collection for future generations. Another family member, Edward's youngest son Andy, is now director of the Deer Lodge Towe Ford Museum and ably applying his own growing knowledge of the collection and Fords in general.

Chapter 9

OPPORTUNITY KNOCKS

There is a unique opportunity for the car enthusiast to become a part of this great project. You can help by visiting the Sacramento and Deer Lodge museums with your family and friends; and after you visit tell more people about it. The Sacramento facility was planned and opened to the public based on faith, the faith that the general public would appreciate and support the public display of this unique part of America's industrial heritage. The California Vehicle Foundation's plans for the Sacramento facility include displaying the cars in dioramas that depict settings that show what the world was like during the time the cars were produced. The entire project needs several millions of dollars to provide these dioramas and additional improvements to the facilities that house the auto collection.

You are also invited to join the California Vehicle Foundation. For a moderate annual membership fee you can help ensure the future of this organization and the continuation of its valuable work. The CVF is able to accept tax deductible donations. The CVF also accepts donations of historically significant vehicles with the reasonable expectation that they will be on display for generations to come. Other donated vehicles will be utilized to generate cash to continue the Foundation's work.

CALIFORNIA VEHICLE FOUNDATION
2200 Front St.
Sacramento, Ca. 95818
(916)442-6802

MEMBERSHIP APPLICATION
for calendar year

N a m e :_____

A d d r e s s :_____

City, State, Zip:_____

Telephone:_____

___NEW   ___RENEWAL

Type of Membership (Check one)
All members receive a newsletter

___$5,000 Benefactor   ___$1,000 Heritage
___$ 500 Classic   ___$ 250 Sustaining
___$ 100 Century   ___$ 50 Particip.
___$ 25 Reg./Family   ___$ 15 Sr. Citizen
___$ 15 Student   (Age 65 or over)

___ I wish to make a tax-deducatable gift as follows
(vehicles, literature, memorabilia etc.)

_____

APPENDIX

YEAR	MODEL	BODY STYLE	ACQUIRED	MUSEUM
1903	A	Runabout	1980	Sac.
1903	A	Runabout	1961	DL
1903		Cadillac	1984	Sac.
1904	B	Touring	1971	Sac.
1905	C	Runabout	1972	Sac.
1905	F	Touring	1962	Sac.
1906	N	Runabout	1973	Sac.
1906	N	Runabout	1962	DL
1906	K	Touring	1973	Sac.
1907	K	Roadster 6—40	1975	DL
1907	R	Runabout	1967	Sac.
1908	S	Runabout	1967	Sac.
1908	S	Runabout	1972	DL
1908	T	Touring	1971	Sac.
1909	T	Touring	1966	Sac.
1909	T	Tourister	1977	DL
1910	T	Torpedo	1978	Sac.
1910	T	Touring	1967	DL
1911	T	Runabout	1979	DL
1911	T	Torpedo w/doors	1965	DL
1911	T	Torpedo w/o doors	1964	Sac.
1911	T	Touring	1955	Sac.
1911	T	Town Car	1978	Sac.
1912	T	Touring	1965	Sac.
1913	T	Runabout	1967	Sac.
1913	T	Touring	1974	Sac.
1913	T	Depot Hack	1973	DL
1913	T	Express Wagon	1968	Sac.
1914	T	Speedster	1978	DL
1914	T	Runabout	1961	Sac.
1914	T	Touring	1958	DL
1915	T	Town Car	1975	Sac.
1915	T	Runabout	1966	Sac.
1915	T	Couplet	1963	Sac.
1916	T	Touring	1961	Sac.
1917	T	Truck	1963	Sac.
1917	T	Touring	1961	Sac.
1917	T	Canadian Touring	1984	DL

YEAR	MODEL	BODY STYLE	ACQUIRED	MUSEUM
1918	T	Touring	1973	Sac.
1919	Stanley	Steamer, Touring	1974	DL
1919	T	Center Door Sedan	1960	Sac.
1920	T	Touring	1977	Sac.
1921	T	Roadster	1963	Sac.
1922	Lincoln	H. Ford's Lin.Camper	0	DL
1922	Lincoln	Leland Lincoln Sedan	0	DL
1922	T	Coupe	1963	Sac.
1923	Lincoln	4 Door Sedan	0	DL
1923	TT	C−Cab Truck	1977	DL
1923	T	Roadster	1952	Sac.
1923	TT	Fire Truck	1980	Sac.
1923	T	Fordor Sedan	1970	Sac.
1924	T	Touring	1958	Sac.
1925	T	Coupe	1960	Sac.
1925	T	Racer	1963	DL
1925	Lincoln	Doctor's Coupe	1978	DL
1926	T	Tudor Sedan	1978	Sac.
1926	TT	Grain Truck	1958	Sac.
1926	T	Roadster	1964	Sac.
1926	T	Coupe	1960	Sac.
1926	Lincoln	Dual Cowl Phaeton	1971	DL
1926	T	Fordor Sedan	1954	DL
1927	T	Speedster	1973	DL
1927	T	Touring	1960	Sac.
1928	AR	Tudor Sedan	1970	Sac.
1928	A	Sport Coupe	1975	Sac.
1928	AR	Phaeton	1972	Sac.
1928	A	Roadster	1979	Sac.
1928	A	Coupe	1960	Sac.
1928	A	Pickup	1973	Sac.
1928	Chevrolet	Coach	1980	Sac.
1929	A	Briggs Sedan	1976	Sac.
1929	A	Town Car	1973	Sac.
1929	A	Town Sedan	1961	DL
1929	A	Sedan Delivery	0	DL
1929	A	Special Coupe	0	DL
1929	AA	Stake Truck	0	Sac.

YEAR	MODEL	BODY STYLE	ACQUIRED	MUSEUM
1929	A	Station Wagon	1975	Sac.
1929	A	Station Wagon	1975	DL
1929	A	Mail Truck	1984	Sac.
1929	A	Open Cab Pickup	1956	Sac.
1929	A	Roadster	1958	DL
1929	A	Roadster	1979	Sac.
1929	A	Phaeton	1962	Sac.
1930	A	Town Sedan	1973	Sac.
1930	A	Tudor Sedan	1962	Sac.
1930	A	Station Wagon	1973	Sac.
1930	A	Coupe	1969	Sac.
1930	A	Deluxe Phaeton	1978	Sac.
1930	A	Deluxe Phaeton	0	DL
1930	A	Deluxe Roadster	0	Sac.
1930	A	Phaeton, 4−Dr	1981	Sac.
1930	A	Pickup	1969	Sac.
1931	A	Cabriolet	1975	Sac.
1931	A	Town Sedan	1980	Sac.
1931	A	Tudor Sedan	1982	Sac.
1931	A	Victoria	1973	Sac.
1931	AA	Mail Truck	0	Sac.
1931	A	Roadster	0	DL
1931	A	Coupe	0	DL
1931	A	Deluxe Phaeton	1979	Sac.
1931	A	Deluxe Roadster	0	Sac.
1931	A	Phaeton	1965	Sac.
1931	A	Pickup	1973	Sac.
1931	A	Pickup	1980	DL
1931	AA	Fire Truck	1975	Sac.
1931	A−400	Convertible Sedan	1969	Sac.
1931	A−400	Convertible Sedan	0	DL
1932	B	5−W Coupe	0	Sac.
1932	V8	Cabriolet	0	Sac.
1932	V8	Sport Coupe	1982	Sac.
1932	B	Open Cab Pickup	0	Sac.
1932	B	Roadster	1964	DL
1932	V8	Deluxe Phaeton	1980	Sac.
1932	B	Deluxe Tudor Sedan	0	Sac.

YEAR	MODEL	BODY STYLE	ACQUIRED	MUSEUM
1932	B	Deluxe St. Wagon	1986	Sac.
1932	V8	Fordor Sedan	1973	Sac.
1932	B−400	Convertible Sedan	1969	Sac.
1933	V8	Cabriolet	1969	Sac.
1933	CC	Truck	0	DL
1933	V8	Station Wagon	1967	Sac.
1933	V8	Roadster	1968	Sac.
1933	V8	Coupe, 3−W	0	Sac.
1933	V8	Phaeton	1978	Sac.
1933	V8	Fordor Sedan	1978	Sac.
1933	Auburn	Cabriolet	0	DL
1934	V8	Cabriolet	0	DL
1934	V8	Tudor Sedan	1983	Sac.
1934	V8	Deluxe Roadster	1979	Sac.
1934	C	Phaeton	1968	Sac.
1934	V8	Phaeton	0	DL
1935	V8	Cabriolet	1962	Sac.
1935	V8	Roadster	1962	Sac.
1935	V8	Phaeton	1977	Sac.
1935	V8	Pickup 1/2 Ton	1981	Sac.
1935	V8	Fordor Sedan	1965	Sac.
1936	V8	Cabriolet	0	Sac.
1936	V8	Truck, 1 1/2 Ton	1976	DL
1936	Lincoln	Zephyr Sedan	1975	DL
1936	V8	Station Wagon	1980	Sac.
1936	V8	Roadster	0	Sac.
1936	V8	Deluxe Fordor Sedan	0	Sac.
1936	V8	Phaeton	1972	Sac.
1936	V8	Convertible Sedan	0	Sac.
1937	V8	Cabriolet	0	Sac.
1937	V8	Tudor Sedan	0	Sac.
1937	Lincoln	Zephyr Sedan	0	DL
1937	V8	Roadster	1977	Sac.
1937	V8	Convertible Sedan	1968	Sac.
1937	V8	Coupe	1969	Sac.
1937	V8	Phaeton	0	Sac.
1937	V8	Pickup 1/2 Ton	1979	Sac.
1938	V8	Tudor Sedan	1979	Sac.

YEAR	MODEL	BODY STYLE	ACQUIRED	MUSEUM
1938	V8	Deluxe Phaeton	1977	Sac.
1938	V8	Deluxe Station Wagon	1970	Sac.
1938	V8	Fordor	1975	DL
1938	V8	Club Cabriolet	0	DL
1939	Mercury	Tudor Sedan	1974	Sac.
1939	V8	Tudor Sedan	1977	Sac.
1939	Lincoln	Zephyr 3 Pass. Coupe	1981	DL
1939	V8	Standard Coupe	1976	DL
1939	V8	Del. Conv. Sedan	1977	Sac.
1939	V8	Pickup	0	DL
1939	V8	Deluxe Tudor Sedan	1977	Sac.
1940	V8	Tudor Sedan	1978	Sac.
1940	V8	Deluxe Coupe	1978	Sac.
1940	V8	Deluxe Station Wagon	0	Sac.
1940	V8	Deluxe Tudor Sedan	0	DL
1940	V8	Club Cabriolet	0	DL
1941	V8	Sup. Del. Club Coupe	0	Sac.
1941	V8	Sup. Del. Fordor Sedan	1973	Sac.
1941	8N	Pickup, 4 cyl.	1977	Sac.
1941	V8	Deluxe Station Wagon	1982	DL
1942	"6"	Tudor Sedan	1976	Sac.
1942	V8	Tudor Sedan	1977	DL
1942	"6"	Ford Jeep	1980	Sac.
1946	V8	Sup. Del. Conv. Coupe	0	Sac.
1946	V8	Fordor Sedan	1983	Sac.
1946	Lincoln	Continental	0	DL
1947	V8	Tudor Sedan	1977	Sac.
1947	V8	Sportsman	1982	Sac.
1947	Lincoln	Continental	0	DL
1948	V8	Sup. Del. Fordor Sedan	1978	Sac.
1948	"6"	Mail Truck	0	DL
1949	V8	Station Wagon	0	Sac.
1950	V8	Fordor Sedan	1979	Sac.
1950	Lincoln	Cosmopolitan	1971	DL
1951	V8	Crestline Tudor Sedan	1983	DL
1951	V8	Custom Tudor Sedan	1977	Sac.
1952	V8	Tudor Sedan	1981	Sac.

YEAR	MODEL	BODY STYLE	ACQUIRED	MUSEUM
1954	Lincoln	Capri Sedan	0	DL
1955	V8	Crown Victoria	0	DL
1955		Thunderbird	1974	Sac.
1955	Lincoln	Capri Coupe	1973	DL
1956	Lincoln	4 Door Sedan	0	DL
1957	Lincoln	Premiere	1979	DL
1957	V8	Fairlaine Ret. Hardtop	0	Sac.
1958	V8	Fairlane Fordor Sedan	1977	DL
1958	Edsel	Citation Sedan	1976	Sac.
1959	Edsel	Station Wagon	0	Sac.
1959	Lincoln	Premiere	1980	DL
1960	Edsel	4—Door Sedan	0	Sac.
1960	V8	Fordor Sedan	1977	Sac.
1960		Galaxie	0	Sac.
1961		Falcon	0	Sac.
1964	V8	Galaxie Convertible	1982	Sac.
1965		Mustang Convertible	1978	Sac.
1967	Lincoln	4 Door Sedan	0	DL
1967		Falcon	1978	Sac.
1968	Lincoln	2 Door Sedan	0	DL
1970	Lincoln	Mark III Coupe	0	DL
1970		Maverick	0	Sac.
1971		Pinto	0	Sac.
1978		Thunderbird	1982	DL

* Acquired "0" indicates insufficient information available at time of public-
ation to determine exact year this vehicle was added to the collection.

** Museum "Sac." = Sacramento, California; "DL" = Deer Lodge, Montana.

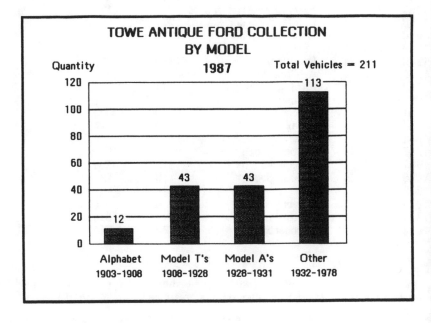

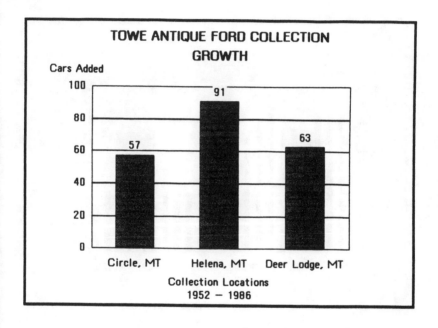

TOWE ANTIQUE FORD COLLECTION GROWTH

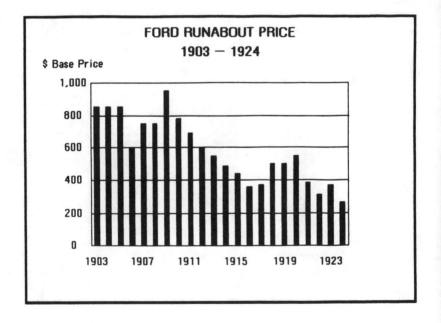

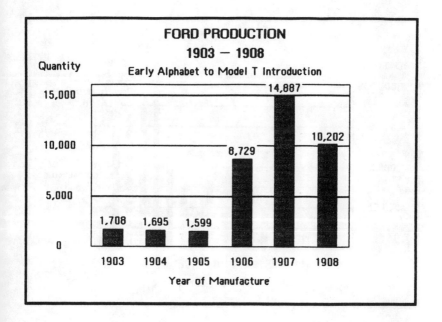

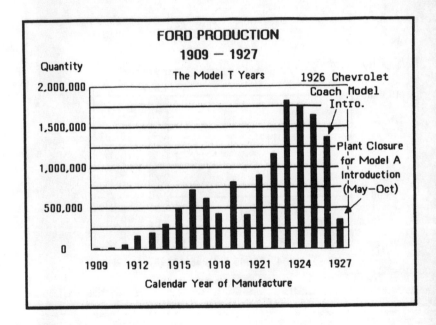